My Lifebook Journal

A Workbook for Children in Foster Care

THERESE ACCINELLI, LMFT

Instant Help Books
A Division of New Harbinger Publications, Inc.

Publisher's Note

This publication is designed to provide accurate and authoritative information in regard to the subject matter covered. It is sold with the understanding that the publisher is not engaged in rendering psychological, financial, legal, or other professional services. If expert assistance or counseling is needed, the services of a competent professional should be sought.

Distributed in Canada by Raincoast Books

Copyright © 2008 by Therese Accinelli
              Instant Help Books
              A Division of New Harbinger Publications, Inc.
              5674 Shattuck Avenue
              Oakland, CA 94609
              www.newharbinger.com

Cover design by Amy Shoup

Cover photo is a model used for illustrative purposes only.

Printed in the United States of America

Library of Congress Cataloging-in-Publication Data on file with publisher

10   09   08

10 9 8 7 6 5 4 3 2 1

First printing

Contents

A Note to Adults   v

Introduction   vii

Activity 1 My Self-Portrait   1

Activity 2 When I Was Born   4

Activity 3 My Medical Record   7

Activity 4 My Biological Family   10

Activity 5 My Foster Family   13

Activity 6 My Very Best Friend   16

Activity 7 My Address Book   19

Activity 8 The Schools I Have Attended   22

Activity 9 My List of Favorites   25

Activity 10 The Person I Admire the Most   28

Activity 11 Feeling Proud   31

Activity 12 Very Random Questions   35

Activity 13 My Many Feelings   38

Activity 14 Managing My Anger   41

Activity 15 Anger Emergency Kit   45

Activity 16 The Truth About Lying   48

Activity 17 People Care About Me   53

Activity 18 Things I'd Like to Have   56

Activity 19 My Grown-Up Dreams for the Future   60

Activity 20 My Earliest Memory   63

Activity 21 My Best Birthday Memory   66

Activity 22 My Best Easter Memory   69

Activity 23 My Best Summer Memory   72

Activity 24 My Best Vacation Memory   75

Activity 25 My Best Camping Memory   78

Activity 26 My Best School Memory   81

Activity 27 My Best Halloween Memory   84

Activity 28 My Best Thanksgiving Memory   87

Activity 29 My Best Christmas Memory   90

Activity 30 My Best Anything Memory   93

Activity 31 What's on Your Mind   95

Activity 32 Helping Hand   98

Activity 33 Loving Heart   101

Activity 34 Upset Stomach   104

Activity 35 Stomp with Your Feet   107

Activity 36 Clap with Your Hands   110

Activity 37 Picture Journal   113

Activity 38 Collage Fun   116

      My Happy Collage   117

      My Sad Collage   118

      My Angry Collage   119

      My Calm Collage   120

      My Room Collage   121

      My Animal Collage   122

      My Fun Stuff Collage   123

      My Yard Collage   124

      My Favorite Things Collage   125

      A Collage About Me   126

A Note to Adults

Being in foster care is difficult for all children, even when they are placed in a good home with loving and experienced caretakers. In fact researchers tell us that being away from one's parents—even for the best of reasons—is the single most significant stress for children. But this thoughtfully written workbook by Therese Accinelli, a therapist with years of experience in working with children in foster care, can help children build the resiliency skills they need to adjust to almost any new situation.

The book is designed to be a journal for children that will simultaneously help them make sense out of their current living situation and prepare them for the inevitable changes and challenges of growing up. The book will help children explore their feelings (particularly their anger), hold on to good memories, and develop a positive attitude toward themselves and others.

The activities in this workbook can be used in counseling sessions or as "therapeutic homework" between counseling sessions. While the activities themselves will have a positive benefit, the book will be most helpful when combined with the positive support and guidance of adults. The activities in this book are wonderful tools to help children heal from past hurts, but healing does not come from any book; it comes in the context of warm and supportive relationships.

As you help a child with the activities in this book, you will probably find out that it is difficult for children to talk about certain issues. Never force a child to talk if he or she doesn't want to. The best way to get children to open up is to be a good role model. Talk about *your* thoughts, feelings, and experiences as they relate to each activity, stressing the positive ways that *you* cope with problems. Even if a child doesn't say a thing back, your words will have an impact on his or her behavior.

As you use this workbook, you must always remember to remain patient and respectful of a child's feelings. Many adults have a tendency to want to put difficult feelings and experiences in the past, but children need to lead the way toward their own healing Fortunately, most children have a great capacity for growth and self-acceptance. Your time and caring will make all the difference.

Sincerely,

Lawrence E. Shapiro, PhD

Introduction

Dear Reader,

I have written this book especially for you. I hope that you will find this book helpful as you live, learn, and adjust to your placement in foster care. I realize that placement in foster care can be difficult for many reasons. There are many changes that take place in your life that require your cooperation and understanding. Many of the changes are things over which you have no control. You must learn to adjust to a lot of new things such as a different family, environment, group of friends, set of rules, school, and community, to name a few. Sometimes these changes can bring about a wide range of feelings. Feelings such as sadness, fear, and anger can sometimes interfere with your ability to feel happy, adjust well, and feel successful in life.

It is my hope that after completing the activities from *My Lifebook Journal: A Workbook for Children in Foster Care*, you will begin to have a better understanding about yourself, your family and how you can adjust to the changes in your life.

My hope is that you will have fun, use creativity, and enjoy yourself while completing pictures about your life, hopes, dreams, and wishes. These activities show that it doesn't have to hurt or be hard to heal and have fun.

Best wishes on your Lifebook Journey,

Therese Accinelli

"I can shake off everything if I write; my sorrows disappear; my courage is reborn...."

—Anne Frank
Anne Frank: The Diary of a Young Girl

Assignment

Draw a picture of yourself and answer questions about your drawing.

Drawing can be a great way to express yourself. As the artist, you can create your outcome. You select the colors, style, and image to draw! This is your opportunity to capture your own image and express how you might be feeling through artwork.

You can use pen, pencil, crayon, marker, pastels, or paint to complete your self-portrait.

Helpful Hints

It might be helpful for you to look at a photograph of yourself or look in a mirror while drawing your self-portrait.

Take a few minutes before you begin your drawing to clear your mind of any negative thoughts about yourself or your artistic abilities.

Remember

Even if your drawing doesn't turn out exactly as you wanted it, it is uniquely your own. And for that reason alone, it's great!

Extra-Credit Assignment

Photocopy and attach the most recent picture of yourself to this page.

My Self-Portrait

Draw your self-portrait in the frame below.

Looking at your self-portrait, briefly describe what you are thinking, feeling, and doing.

_____

_____

_____

_____

All About Me

Directions

Complete the sentences below:

My full name is: _____

My birth date is: _____

The school I attend is: _____

Currently, I am in the _____ grade.

The color of my eyes is: _____

The color of my skin is: _____

The color of my hair is: _____

My height is: _____

My weight is: _____

Assignment

Complete the information about your birth.

You probably don't remember when you were born, but from the moment of your birth, information about you was put in writing.

When you were first born, the doctors and nurses who delivered you documented your time of birth, weight, and length. They also conducted special tests called APGARs to make sure your body parts and reflexes were working right.

Of course, you were too little to remember all of the information about your birth. Because of this, you will probably need to get some help with this information.

Helpful Hints

1. Ask your biological parent, social worker, or other relative to help you complete the information on the next page.

2. Get a copy of your birth certificate and copy the information directly from your birth certificate.

If you don't have a copy of your birth certificate, you can ask your social worker, biological parents, foster parents, or counselor to help you.

Extra-Credit Assignment

Obtain and attach a photocopy of your birth certificate to this page.

When

_____

(Write in your name here.)

Was Born

First name: _____ Middle name: _____

Last name: _____

Date of birth: _____

City, state, country of birth: _____

_____

Name of hospital: _____

Time of birth: _____

Weight at birth: _____

Length at birth: _____

Directions

In the space provided below, glue or tape in a baby picture of yourself. If you do not have a copy of your baby picture, draw a picture of what you think you might have looked like as a baby.

Assignment

Complete the information about your medical history.

Your medical history can help provide you and your foster parents with important information that can help keep you safe and healthy.

Your biological parents, current and previous foster parents, school staff, medical doctors, mental health clinicians, or social workers can help you get information about your medical record.

Your biological parents or social worker can help you get a copy of your birth record from the hospital where you were born. Your birth record has even more detailed information about your birth than your birth certificate.

Your birth record includes notes from the doctors and nurses who took care of you and your biological mother after you were born.

You might not have all of your medical information handy as you complete the assignment. That's okay—just complete as much of the information as you know.

Extra-Credit Assignments

1. Obtain a photocopy of your immunization record and attach it to this page.

2. Obtain a copy of your birth record and attach it to this page.

My Medical Record

My full name: _____

My date of birth: _____

My biological mother's name: _____

My biological father's name: _____

My place of birth: _____

Blood type: _____

Allergies: _____

_____

Serious injuries: _____

_____

Hospitalizations: _____

_____

Scars or birthmarks: _____

_____

Current medications and dosage: _____

_____

Directions

Complete the answers to the questions below. Ask for help from adults who've known you since you were little.

Illnesses

1. Did you ever have the chicken pox, or a bad case of the flu or were you ever really sick with another illness? Write about your illness.

   _____

   _____

2. Were you ever in the hospital for an operation or an illness?

   _____

Milestones

1. At what age did you first sit up by yourself? _____

2. At what age did you say your first word? _____

3. What was your first word? _____

4. At what age did you start to crawl? _____

5. At what age did you start to walk? _____

6. When did you lose your first tooth? _____

Activity 4   My Biological Family

Assignment

Complete the information about your biological family.

Everyone has biological parents: a biological mother and a biological father. They will always remain your biological parents, even if you are placed in long-term foster care or you are adopted.

Some children know their biological mother and father very well and continue to see them on a regular basis while they are placed in foster care.

However, some children may not know their biological parents well at all. Perhaps a birth parent died, went to jail, or no one knows where he or she is living.

Regardless of the amount of contact you may have with your biological family, they are the only set of biological parents you will ever have. For that reason alone, they are an important part of your childhood and your life.

In the next assignment, you will be asked to complete information about your biological family and draw a family portrait.

Extra-Credit Assignment

Attach a photocopy of a photograph of your biological family to this page.

My Biological Family

My name: _____

Biological family address: _____

_____

Phone #: _____

My biological parents' names are: _____

and _____

My grandparents' names are: _____

and _____

My aunts, uncles, and other relatives are: _____

_____

My biological siblings are: _____

_____

I also lived with: _____

The pets are: _____

Fun times I remember: _____

_____

Sad times I remember: _____

_____

Directions

Complete the questions below.

List three things that you like about your biological home:

1. _____

2. _____

3. _____

List three things that you would like to change about your biological home:

1. _____

2. _____

3. _____

Below, draw a picture of your biological family. Please label all family members in your drawing. If you have one, you may also glue in a photograph of your biological family.

Assignment

Complete the information about your foster family.

Placement in foster care can be a big change in your life. Adjusting to this change can take time, but it usually becomes easier as time passes and you get to know your foster family better.

If you have lived in more than one foster home, you might want to complete a *My Foster Family* page for each of the different foster homes in which you lived.

A lot of children think that the reason that they are in foster care is because they did something wrong. THAT IS NOT TRUE!

Adults are responsible for the well-being of children, and when something goes wrong, the court steps in to help.

Sometimes the court decides that children can return home with their biological family, and other times the court decides that children need to remain in foster care until their parents are ready and able to take care of them.

Occasionally, the children's parents are unable or unwilling to care for them. When this happens, the court makes long-term plans for the children, such as long-term foster care placement, legal guardianship, or adoption.

Extra-Credit Assignment

Attach a photocopy of a photograph of your foster family to this page.

My Foster Family

My name: _____

Foster family address: _____

_____

Phone #: _____

My foster parents' names are: _____

and _____

I also live with (siblings, foster relatives): _____

_____

The pets are: _____

I was placed in foster care on: _____

because: _____

_____

_____

_____

_____

Optional Activity

Complete the questions below.

List three things that you like about your foster home:

1. _____

2. _____

3. _____

List three things that you would like to change about your foster home:

1. _____

2. _____

3. _____

Below, draw a picture of your foster family. Please label all family members in your drawing. If you have one, you may also glue in a photograph of your foster family.

Activity 6   My Very Best Friend

Assignment

Identify what you value in a friend, what kind of friend you are
to others, and how to become a better friend.

Everyone needs at least one good friend. You probably feel comfortable and relaxed when you are around your friends. Friends have a way of making you smile when you're feeling down.

However, friendship requires work, and building friendships takes time. This can be especially difficult if you've moved recently or changed schools. The assignment on the following pages should assist you in building good friendship skills. Remember, the quickest way to make a friend is by being a good friend to others.

Below are a few inspirational quotes about friendship.

"I get by with a little help from my friends."
— John Lennon

"A real friend is one who walks in when the rest of the world walks out."
—Walter Winchell

"My best friend is the one who brings out the best in me."
—Henry Ford

"A friend is someone who knows all about you, and loves you anyway."
—Anonymous

Extra-Credit Assignment

Photocopy a picture of your best friend (or draw a picture of your friend) and attach it to this page.

1. My very best friend is:

   _____

2. We met at

   when I was _____ years old.

3. I like my friend because: _____

   _____

   _____

4. I know my friend likes me because: _____

   _____

   _____

5. Some of the fun things we do together are: _____

   _____

   _____

6. Other friends I have are: _____

   _____

7. My best friend's address and phone number are: _____

   _____

   _____

My Best Friend

Directions

Answer the questions below.

1. Circle the qualities that you value in a friend.

   loyal   nice   funny   good dancer   good manners

   polite   energetic   accepting   good listener   friendly

   brave   kind   honest   understanding   helpful

   truthful   takes turns   shares   secret keeper   popular

2. Do you have the same qualities that you circled above?

   Circle one: YES   NO

3. Why or why not?

   _____

   _____

   _____

4. What are some ways you could be a better friend to others?

   _____

5. Interview your friend and ask what he or she likes the best about you. Write his or her response here:

   _____

   _____

Assignment

**Complete the names, addresses, and phone numbers of
important people in your life.**

All children have important people in their lives. Some of these important people are
children, like friends and classmates. Other important people are adults, like biological
parents, foster parents, teachers, social workers, attorneys, and counselors.

There are times when you may need to call upon these important people for help or
just to talk. Having their names, addresses, and phone numbers together in one place
helps you stay organized and makes it easy to find this information if you need it.

When you add their information to the following page, be sure to include their first,
middle, and last names and all phone numbers, such as work phone numbers, home
phone numbers, cellular phone numbers, and pager numbers. If you find that you have
more important people in your life than will fit on one page, you may need to make
more than one copy of the following page.

Tip

If you are having a difficult time obtaining phone numbers of relatives, ask your social
worker or biological family to assist you.

Extra-Credit Assignment

Create a list of ten or more important people in your life. Attach the list to this page.

Directions

Please use this list to keep track of important people in your life. These people might include your friends, foster family, biological family, attorney, social worker, or counselor.

Name: _____

Address: _____

Phone numbers: _____

Name: _____

Address: _____

Phone numbers: _____

Name: _____

Address: _____

Phone numbers: _____

Name: _____

Address: _____

Phone numbers: _____

Finding the Important People

Directions

Complete the word search by circling as many words as you can find below. The words may be hidden vertically, horizontally, or diagonally.

Important People

friend	classmate	teacher	social worker
counselor	foster mother	foster father	relative
attorney	babysitter	brother	sister
aunt	uncle	grandpa	grandma
mentor	tutor	minister	neighbor

S	A	U	N	C	L	E	B	C	T	E	C	T	B	R	O	T	H	E	R	E
O	D	E	U	O	Q	T	H	A	S	B	L	C	A	N	A	S	E	B	E	S
C	O	U	N	S	E	L	O	R	N	C	A	T	T	O	R	N	E	Y	L	U
I	F	B	V	N	M	W	Z	D	E	M	S	F	G	M	F	H	J	T	A	W
A	W	A	L	E	R	I	R	L	F	I	S	H	S	N	O	N	R	T	T	T
L	G	B	S	R	M	U	S	T	O	N	M	P	R	Q	S	E	L	O	I	M
W	A	Y	U	M	S	E	K	C	S	I	A	M	T	D	T	I	W	S	V	I
O	H	S	R	O	F	J	N	L	M	S	T	U	O	Z	E	G	S	X	E	N
R	S	I	E	N	R	T	W	T	O	T	E	S	N	Y	R	H	T	T	D	H
K	I	T	Y	H	I	E	F	Y	O	E	Y	G	V	T	F	B	A	Z	E	M
E	R	T	R	T	E	A	C	H	E	R	C	T	R	X	A	O	B	T	O	R
R	J	E	A	S	N	T	M	S	H	I	H	U	O	Q	T	R	H	W	V	G
X	G	R	A	N	D	P	A	C	D	R	L	T	R	M	H	R	C	P	E	M
K	Z	L	A	M	E	N	I	O	L	P	N	O	S	W	E	F	O	T	K	A
Y	F	O	S	T	E	R	M	O	T	H	E	R	M	G	R	A	N	D	M	A

Activity 8

The Schools I Have Attended

Assignment

Document information about the schools, teachers, friends, and memories that you have for each grade level.

While growing up, children spend a lot of time in school—about thirty hours each week. And that's not even counting homework! School is an important part of a child's life and teaches many things.

School teaches children basic academic information like reading, writing, and math. It also teaches them about life—things such as getting along with others, learning to play fair, and learning to deal with disappointments.

School can be challenging for children in foster care placement who move frequently. When children move to different homes, they usually change schools. These frequent changes can disrupt learning, hurt your grades, and make it difficult to have good friends.

In this assignment you will be asked to reflect upon all your years of schooling and list the schools that you attended, the teachers you had, and the friends you made.

Hint

If you move frequently and/or can't remember names of schools or teachers, try looking at past report cards. Or you can ask family members or your social worker for help.

Extra-Credit Assignment

Photocopy your school report cards and attach them to this page.

The Schools I Have Attended

Kindergarten: _____

Teachers' names: _____

1st Grade: _____

Teachers' names: _____

2nd Grade: _____

Teachers' names: _____

3rd Grade: _____

Teachers' names: _____

4th Grade: _____

Teachers' names: _____

5th Grade: _____

Teachers' names: _____

6th Grade: _____

Teachers' names: _____

7th Grade: _____

Teachers' names: _____

Directions

Complete the information on this page up to the grade you are in now.

Kindergarten friends and memories: _____

_____

Grades 1-2 friends and memories: _____

_____

Grades 3-4 friends and memories: _____

_____

Grades 5-6 friends and memories: _____

_____

Grades 7-8 friends and memories: _____

_____

As a student, I rate myself as (circle one):

Poor   Below average   Average   Above average   Excellent

What was your favorite grade level? _____

What or who was it that made it your favorite grade? _____

_____

_____

Assignment

Complete the list of your favorite things on the following two pages.

Everyone has favorites—from colors to clothes to classes. The things that make up our list of favorites are called our *preferences*. Preferences are the things that we like the most. Our preferences make us unique as individuals and bring us together with our friends. Have you ever noticed that people with similar interests like to spend time with each other?

How many people in your life know about your list of favorites? Do you share this information with your friends, biological family, foster parents, foster siblings, social worker, or teachers? If you answered "no" about any of these people, you might consider sharing with them.

When you let other people know what your preferences are, you are actually taking the first step toward getting your needs met. This list of favorites can be especially helpful to foster parents if you have recently moved. Consider giving your foster parents a copy of this list after you complete the assignment.

Extra-Credit Assignment

Ask a friend or someone in your family to complete their list of favorites. You can make extra copies of the next two pages to do this.

My List of Favorites

My favorite color is:

_____

My favorite animal is:

_____

My favorite food is:

_____

My favorite ice cream flavor is:

_____

Paste a picture of yourself doing one of your favorite things here.

My favorite actor is: _____

My favorite actress is: _____

My favorite movie is: _____

My favorite TV show is: _____

My favorite cartoon character is: _____

My favorite singer is: _____

My favorite candy bar is: _____

My favorite class at school is: _____

My favorite outfit is: _____

_____

My favorite room of the house is: _____

My favorite relative is: _____

My favorite toy or game is: _____

My favorite place to go is: _____

My favorite song is: _____

My favorite snack is: _____

My favorite book is: _____

My favorite sport is: _____

My favorite fruit is:_____

Activity 10

The Person I Admire the Most

Assignment

Complete the information below about the person whom you admire the most and create a trophy for that person.

Definition: Admire

To admire is to regard a person or thing with wonder and approval. A person whom you "admire the most" is someone whom you see as a hero. This can be someone famous or someone who is very important in your life.

This assignment challenges you to think about a person whom you admire the most and define what those qualities are. People we admire usually have had a powerful affect on us, and our lives have been changed in a positive way by knowing these people.

Sometimes people we have never met but have only read about can have a powerful affect on us. We might be able to understand their life situations or admire them for what they have done for others.

Other people we admire are people we see on a regular basis like a parent, counselor,+ or teacher. Their presence and guidance has made positive changes in our lives.

Extra-Credit Assignment

Photocopy a picture of the person you admire the most and attach it to this page.

The Person I Admire the Most

The person I admire most is: _____

because: _____

_____

_____

When I grow up, I want to be:_____

_____

because: _____

_____

_____

List three more heroes or people you admire:

1. _____

    because: _____

2. _____

    because: _____

3. _____

    because: _____

Directions

Color in the trophy below for the person that you admire the most. Make sure to write an inscription.

Write a few lines stating what you would say to the person you admire the most if you were to give him or her this trophy at an award ceremony.

_____

_____

_____

_____

Assignment

Identify the things that you feel most proud of about yourself.
Record your thoughts and feelings about pride.

How you feel about yourself is part of your self-esteem. When you increase your self-esteem, you increase your feelings of happiness and take steps toward making your life better.

Pride or feeling proud is an example of a feeling that positively affects your self-esteem. When you do something well, you usually feel proud of yourself.

When you feel proud of your appearance, you take time to make sure that your hair is brushed, your body is washed, and your clothing is clean. When you feel proud of your schoolwork, you take your time reading the directions carefully, writing neatly, and completing the assignment accurately.

Do you take pride in your appearance, your school work, and your behavior?

In this activity you will have the opportunity to list some things about yourself that you are proud of.

Extra-Credit Assignment

Find a test or homework assignment that you feel proud of and make a photocopy of it. Attach it to this page.

Feeling Proud

I think pride means: _____

_____

_____

The dictionary states that pride means: _____

_____

_____

Below, circle the things you feel proud of (circle all that apply):

My abilities at sports	My appearance	My biological family
My culture/ethnicity	My belongings	My community
My race	My personality	My schoolwork
My religion	My talents	My behavior
My country	My foster family	My friends

Write the top three things about yourself that you are most proud of and explain why they are important to you.

1. _____

   because: _____

   _____

2. _____

   because: _____

   _____

3. _____

   because: _____

   _____

A special time I felt proud of myself was: _____

_____

_____

I know other people are proud of me when they say or do the following: _____

_____

_____

Is it possible to be too proud? Circle one: YES   NO

Why or why not? _____

_____

Look in the dictionary and define the following three words:

Conceit: _____

_____

Arrogance: _____

_____

Humility: _____

_____

Below, draw a picture of a time when you felt proud.

```
┌─────────────────────────────────────────┐
│                                         │
│                                         │
│                                         │
│                                         │
│                                         │
│                                         │
│                                         │
│                                         │
│                                         │
│                                         │
│                                         │
│                                         │
└─────────────────────────────────────────┘
```

Assignment

Complete the sentences using the very random sentence
starters on the next page.

Has anyone ever asked you random questions about yourself that seemed to come out of the blue or were unrelated to each other? You may have asked yourself: "What is that person thinking?"

In this exercise you will have the opportunity to answer some very random questions about yourself. A lot of people think that this is fun.

The best part about answering random questions is finding out information about yourself that never would have found out unless the random question was asked.

Using random questions can be a fun way to get to know someone else a little better, too. Some of their answers might surprise you, because you never know what kind of answer you're going to get with a random question.

Extra-Credit Assignment

Make up your own list of random questions. Ask a friend to answer the random questions and write down his or her responses. Attach those responses to this page.

Random Questions

The funniest thing is: _____

_____

Books I like: _____

_____

My favorite physical activity is: _____

If I could be an animal, I'd be a: _____

because: _____

I'm proud of: _____

_____

Some ways I don't take care of myself are: _____

_____

I dream about: _____

_____

A country that I'd like to visit is: _____

The grossest thing is: _____

_____

My bedtime is: _____

The ugliest thing is: _____

Directions

In this exercise, you will be asked to choose between two different things. Once you have made your choice by circling your answers, you will need to explain why you chose the way you did.

1. Would you rather be a fish or a bird?

   Why? _____

   _____

2. Would you rather live in a castle or an amusement park?

   Why? _____

   _____

3. Would you rather eat an insect or moldy bread?

   Why? _____

   _____

4. Would you rather be a famous movie star or a famous singer?

   Why? _____

   _____

5. Would you rather lose your sight or your hearing?

   Why? _____

   _____

Activity 13

My Many Feelings

Assignment

Identify your feelings and learn how you respond when you feel a certain way.

Everyone has feelings. It is very important to express your emotions (another word for feelings) in a healthy way. This allows you and other people to know how you feel. Once you have identified your feelings, you can find a way to work through the situation that caused you to feel that way in the first place.

It is important for you to identify the things that contribute to feeling a certain way. You should be able to answer the following questions about your feelings: When do you feel this way? Where are you when the feelings occur? Why are the feelings occurring? How often do you feel that way? How intense is the feeling? How do you behave when you feel that way?

Some children become overwhelmed or scared of their feelings. Maybe in the past they were discouraged or punished for expressing their feelings in a certain way. They might also feel disconnected from their feelings and need to learn how to identify their feelings now that there is a safe place to do so.

Usually, your body lets you know when you are feeling a specific emotion. When you're feeling angry, you might feel your heart beating quickly, your breathing becoming rapid, and your muscles tightening. This is your body telling you that you are angry.

Extra-Credit Assignment

Cut out five faces from a magazine and label what they might be feeling. Attach the faces to this page.

My Many Feelings

1. I feel happy when: _____

   _____

2. When I am sad I: _____

   _____

3. Some things that make me cry are: _____

   _____

4. I am afraid of: _____

   _____

5. Things that make me laugh are: _____

   _____

6. Things that make me feel angry are: _____

   _____

7. I feel embarrassed when: _____

   _____

8. I feel worried about: _____

   _____

9. Things that make me feel excited are: _____

   _____

My Many Feelings

Directions

Look at the pictures below of the different faces. Write in the feeling word that you think they might be feeling. Use the word bank to help you, if needed.

afraid	angry	anxious	ashamed
bored	confident	confused	depressed
excited	exhausted	ecstatic	frightened
frustrated	guilty	happy	hopeful
jealous	sad	scared	shocked
shy	silly	surprised	worried

Assignment

Learn to identify anger warning signs and use anger management tools.

Many children have a difficult time managing their anger. When you are angry, your body goes into a fight-or-flight response. Your brain responds by releasing chemicals into your bloodstream to assist you in fighting or running away.

The chemicals from your brain cause your body to change in ways that you might not be aware of. In this assignment, you will be asked to identify the warning signs that your body gives you to let you know when you are feeling angry.

Some of the warning signs include rapid breathing, increased pulse rate, and muscle tension. The best way to prevent anger outbursts is to learn how to identify the early anger warning signs.

When you catch yourself feeling angry, you can calm yourself down before your anger escalates.

One way to calm down is by using the S.T.O.P. method. "S.T.O.P." stands for "Stop," "Think," "Options," and "Plan."

> **Stop** first before doing anything.

> **Think** before acting.

> Consider your **Options** for reducing angry feelings.

> Carefully **Plan** what you will do or say next.

Extra-Credit Assignment

The next time you feel angry, use the S.T.O.P. method and log what you did. Attach a copy of your findings to this page.

Directions

Complete the questions below.

Have you ever said or done something while angry that you later regretted:

Circle one: YES   NO

Hint: Practice using "I Statements" when you are feeling angry to avoid saying things you really don't mean.

Example: **I feel** angry
          When you make fun of me
          Because it hurts my feelings

Create your own "I statements" below.

I feel: _____

When: _____

Because: _____

I feel: _____

When: _____

Because: _____

I feel: _____

When: _____

Because: _____

What are the warning signs that you feel in your body when you are angry? Circle all that apply to you:

rapid breathing	clenched teeth	tightened muscles
increased pulse rate	pacing	unclear thoughts
goose bumps	knot in stomach	trembling
flushed face	clenched fists	dry mouth
talking louder	pupils dilating	bulging veins

Directions

Unscramble the letters to solve the ten different, positive anger management tools.
Draw a line to the correct phrase.

1. AWKL WAAY   COUNT TO TEN

2. TIEWR UOBAT TI   BREATHE DEEPLY

3. GREAN NCEAD   TALK IT OUT

4. CSIEEEXR   WALK AWAY

5. ETAEHRB EPELYD   WRITE ABOUT IT

6. OUNDP AYLC   THINK POSITIVE

7. NTCUO OT NTE   EXERCISE

8. LLWOIP REMCSA   POUND CLAY

9. HTKNI OSPIVTIE   PILLOW SCREAM

10. AKLT TI UTO   ANGER DANCE

Choose the three anger management tools that you would be most likely to use when you are feeling angry.

1. _____

2. _____

3. _____

Assignment

Create and use your own Anger Emergency Kit.

Anger is a completely normal emotion that everyone feels. Anger is neither good nor bad, but the way you react and respond to your anger will determine if anger is going to be a problem for you in your life.

If you learn to use positive anger management tools when you feel angry, anger is generally not a problem. However, if you allow your anger to escalate out of control, it usually causes problems for you as well as for other people around you.

In this assignment, you will be asked to create an Anger Emergency Kit. This kit will help you react and respond to anger in ways that will help calm you down. You might have to use several different items in your Anger Emergency Kit before you begin to feel calmer.

Creating this kit should be fun. You will probably need an adult's help purchasing all the items needed for the kit. Use your creativity and make this kit work for you!

Extra-Credit Assignment

Find one small item that will help you remember that the anger feelings will pass. Add this special item to your Anger Emergency Kit. Write down what the special item is and attach it to this page.

Directions

Create your own Anger Emergency Kit.

The Anger Emergency Kit may include the following items:

ITEMS	USE
1. Bubbles	to teach controlled breathing
2. Soft ball	to teach counting (1-10) before acting
3. Play dough	for positive physical outlet
4. Note pad/journal	to write and draw angry feelings
5. Jump rope	for physical exercise as an outlet
6. Latex balloon	for focused breathing
7. Bubble packing wrap	for stress reduction and focus
8. Crayons	anger expression through art work
9. Pen or pencil	to complete assignments in this book
10. Five handouts (see below)	to help you learn about yourself

Five Handouts from This Book

1. Managing My Anger   (Activity # 14)
2. My Many Feelings   (Activity # 13)
3. What's on Your Mind   (Activity # 31)
4. Picture Journal   (Activity # 37)
5. My Self-Portrait   (Activity # 1)

Directions and Guidelines

1. Make your Anger Emergency Kit by using an empty shoe box or a plastic box with a lid. You can use stickers and paint pens to decorate the outside of the box.

2. Keep the Anger Emergency Kit in a central location in the house.

3. Practice each item to help you deal with your anger (*Note:* You may want to ask a grown-up for help with this).

4. Remember two rules for using the Anger Emergency Kit:
   Rule 1: You must not hurt yourself or anyone else.
   Rule 2: You must use all items in the kit for their intended use.

5. Add additional items to the kit if you think they will be useful.

Assignment

Learn to identify the reasons why you lie and how you can rebuild
trust after a lie is told.

Lying occurs when you say something that isn't true. You might lie for a number of different reasons, but the biggest reason is usually fear: the fear of being punished for something you did that was wrong. Lying sometimes protects you from getting into trouble in the short term. But lying has very harmful effects on how people perceive you, trust you, and believe you in the future.

Trust is built when people prove themselves to be honest and reliable. Over time, you can build trust with just about anyone. But when the trust is broken, it might take a while for you to be trusted again.

Maybe someone you care about has hurt you by being untrustworthy. Perhaps they made promises to you that they didn't keep. This is an example of the hurtful effects of a lie.

Remember: A lie slips out quickly and easily, but it's very difficult to take back once it's out.

The Story of Pinocchio

There are several very popular stories about lying. Each one has an important lesson to teach.

One story is called *Pinocchio*. The story is about a puppet who wants to be a real boy. A magic spell is cast on him, and every time he tells a lie, his nose grows a little longer.

What happens in real life when kids tell lies?

_____

_____

Why is it important to be truthful?

_____

_____

_____

When are some times that kids are often not truthful?

_____

_____

_____

Do you think that you are always truthful or do you sometimes tell lies?

_____

_____

_____

The Boy Who Cried Wolf

There is another famous story about a bored shepherd boy who pretended that a wolf was eating his sheep. He cried out "Wolf! Wolf!" and thought it was funny to see the townspeople run to try to help him. He did this three times, even though there was no wolf. Then one day a real wolf came. The boy cried out, but no one came to help him. They were tired of being tricked. The wolf scattered all the sheep, and the boy felt very bad.

Why do you think that the people stopped believing the boy?

_____

_____

_____

Why do you think that the boy lied in the first place?

_____

_____

_____

What do you think is the moral or lesson of this story?

_____

_____

_____

Why Do People Lie?

What is the biggest lie you've ever told? _____

_____

Why do you think you lie? (Circle all that apply.)

1. To get out of trouble

2. To get attention

3. To look important

4. To keep from hurting someone's feelings

5. To protect someone else

6. To get your way

7. To avoid punishment

8. Out of habit

How often do you lie? _____

How do you feel after you tell a lie? _____

_____

_____

When you tell a lie to other people and they find out, how do you think they feel?

_____

_____

Has anyone stopped believing you? Circle one: YES   NO

After you have been caught lying, how do you show that you are a trustworthy person again?

_____

_____

_____

Has someone accused you of telling a lie when you were really telling the truth? What happened?

_____

_____

_____

_____

Assignment

Identify the people in your life that you care about and the people that care about you. Learn how to express your feelings of care and affection toward them.

Through scientific studies, it has been shown that all infants and children need someone to care about them in order to survive and thrive.

Children not only need to have food, clothes, and shelter, but also touch, hugs, and love. Children need to be cared for in a loving way in order to survive.

As children grow older, they continue to need someone to care for them and will seek out those caring adults.

Children who are separated from their parents need to find at least one person who they care about and who cares about them. This caring person can be a relative, neighbor, foster parent, counselor, teacher, or anyone else in their lives that makes them feel special.

We all need someone to care for us. In the next two pages you will have the opportunity to identify people who care about you and people you care about, and to show others that you care about them.

Extra-Credit Assignment

Photocopy or draw a picture of a person who you care about (or who cares about you) and attach it to this page.

Directions

It is very important to have people in your life who care about you. Circle the people in you life that care about you.

Mother	Father	Foster mother	Foster father	Neighbor
Aunt	Uncle	Brother	Sister	Minister/Rabbi
Tutor	Foster brother	Foster sister	Grandmother	Grandfather
Counselor	Friend	Attorney	Teacher	Classmate
Social worker	Judge	Other _____		

How do you know when someone cares about you? _____

_____

_____

List five people that you care about.

1. _____

2. _____

3. _____

4. _____

5. _____

How do you show that you care about these people?

_____

Caring Card

Directions

Make a card for one person that you care about and tell them why you care about them.

You will need

1. A sheet of paper folded in half

2. Crayons or markers to decorate the outside of the card

3. A pen or pencil to write the message inside your card

Below is a sample letter to help you get started:

Dear _____,

(Write the name of the person who cares about you.)

Thank you for caring about me. I care about you too. I know you care about me

because you _____

_____

I really like it when you say "_____"
to me. It makes me feel good inside.

With love,

_____

Activity 18   Things I'd Like to Have

Assignment

Learn to identify the difference between a "want" and a "need."

Everyone has things that they would like to have. These things might include special clothing, toys, games, music CDs, books, food/snacks, or other desired items. These might be items that you can't afford or don't have enough room for. When you can't have them, you are left to wish for and want them.

People never have everything they want, but they can use their imaginations, dreams, and fantasies to create a feeling of what it would be like to have the things they are thinking about. In your fantasies you can own as many things as you would like.

Surprisingly, having something you've wanted can be disappointing. Can you think of a time when you wanted something very badly, but it wasn't what you thought it would be when you finally received it? Think about the toys that were so great to have for a few weeks, but a month later, they cluttered the shelves in your room and now you no longer play with them.

All of these items you're thinking of are WANTS. This means you could probably survive without them. Can you think of things that you NEED? These are things that you must have in order to survive and stay healthy. These are basic things like food, clothing, shelter, and love.

Extra-Credit Assignment

List three things that you could do to get your wants and needs met. Attach the list to this page.

Directions

You can't always get what you want, but it is fun to dream about things that you want. Below, list the things that you would like to have.

Clothing 1. _____

2. _____

3. _____

Toys 1. _____

2. _____

3. _____

Games 1. _____

2. _____

3. _____

Music CDs 1. _____

2. _____

3. _____

Books 1. _____

2. _____

3. _____

Things I'd Like to Have

Food   1. _____

         2. _____

         3. _____

Other things _____

_____

_____

_____

Directions

Look at each of the items below. Circle the item if it is a NEED or underline the item if it is a WANT.

Definition: WANT or NEED

A **WANT** is something that you wish for, but you could live without.

A **NEED** is something that is required for your basic survival, health and wellbeing.

Breakfast	Video game
Jacket	Bike
Bed	Lunch
Water	Shoes
Name-brand shoes	Medicine
Designer jeans	Potato chips
Jewelry	Toothbrush and toothpaste
Blanket	Cellular telephone
Candy bar	Heater

Activity 19

My Grown-Up Dreams for the Future

Assignment

Complete the questions and sentence starters about your future.

Most children dream about what they would like to become when they grow up. Many children want to be firefighters, police officers, ballerinas, astronauts, or famous singers. What do you want to be?

As you continue to grow, it is okay to change your mind often about what you want to be when you grow up. This gives you the opportunity to try out new things and learn new skills.

Can you imagine yourself in the future? What will you and the future look like?

In this exercise, you will have the opportunity to dream and plan out what your future might look like.

As a child, you don't get to be part of the decision-making process for a lot of things. Usually, it is the adults in your life making the decisions. When you grow up, you will have a lot of decisions to make about your life. This is your opportunity to think about your future and decide. Remember—you can always change your mind!

Extra-Credit Assignment

Make two lists on a single sheet of paper. On the left side of the page, write down all the decisions that adults have made in your life that you LIKE. On the right side of the page, list all of the decisions that adults have made in your life that you DO NOT LIKE. Attach the list to this page.

Directions

Fill in the answers to the questions below.

When I grow up, I want to be: _____

_____

because: _____

I want to live in the following city/state/country: _____

_____

When I grow up, I would like to have the following hobbies: _____

_____

_____

I would like to get married? Circle one: YES   NO

Why or why not? _____

I would like to have children? Circle one: YES   NO

If yes, how many? _____

I would like to own the following pets or animals: _____

_____

When I grow up, one thing that I will do differently than my parents did is:_____

_____

_____

Directions

Below, draw a picture of what your house and family might look like. Please label all the people in your drawing.

My Earliest Memory

Assignment

Remember and record your earliest memory from childhood.

Sometimes it is easy to forget things from the past, especially if you have had a lot of changes in your life. As you get older, your memories tend to fade because you add more memories every day.

In this exercise, you will be asked to think about your earliest memory, write it down, and answer some questions about it.

Most children's earliest memories are remembered from the time when they were between the ages of three to five years old. (This is the time period when you might have been in preschool or kindergarten.)

Earliest memories are often, but not always, tied to a powerful event or special occasion. Your earliest memory might be positive, like when you received a special gift or celebrated a fun holiday. However, your earliest memory might be negative, like when someone got hurt or hurt you. Remember that whatever your memory is, it is in the past and is unique to you.

On the next page, you will be asked to write down your earliest memory. It might be helpful for you to sit in a quiet place, close your eyes, breathe deeply, and think back to a time when you were younger.

My Earliest Memory

1 My earliest memory was when I was _____ years old.

2. The following people were present:

_____

_____

3. Briefly describe the memory:

_____

_____

_____

4. The most important part of my memory:

_____

_____

_____

5. The sights, smells, and sounds I remember are:

_____

_____

6. When I think about this memory, I feel:

_____

_____

Optional Activity

Share the activity on the previous page with someone else. Ask them to share their earliest memory with you and write down their response.

1. I shared this memory with: _____

2. Their comments about my memory were: _____

   _____

3. The memory that they shared with me was: _____

   _____

Below, draw a picture of your earliest memory. Please label all the people in your drawing.

Activity 21   My Best Birthday Memory

Assignment

Remember and record your best birthday memory.

Birthdays are usually happy occasions. All year long you probably look forward to that special day that is yours alone to celebrate. For most children, it feels great to be honored and recognized on this day. Another year older means another candle in the birthday cake and another milestone met.

Sometimes there is even a birthday party held in your honor! Cake, ice cream, games, friends, and family are often part of the celebration. Maybe you received a special present or were allowed to choose a special place to go with friends or family.

The way in which birthdays are celebrated is part of a family tradition. Tradition is the way in which parents hand down beliefs and customs to their children. Different families and cultures celebrate birthdays in different ways.

For example, Mexican families have a big "fiesta," which means "party" in Spanish. They have cake, ice cream, music, dancing, and a "piñata" filled with candy and small prizes. Friends and relatives are always invited.

Extra-Credit Assignment

Imagine yourself in the future as a parent. Write down the birthday traditions that you would like to pass along to your children and attach them to this page.

My Best Birthday Memory

1. My best birthday memory was when I was _____ years old.

2. The following people were present:

   _____

   _____

   _____

3. It was the best because:

   _____

   _____

4. The best gift I received was:

   _____

   _____

5. The sights, smells, and sounds I remember are:

   _____

   _____

6. When I think about this memory, I feel: _____

   because: _____

   _____

Directions

Share this birthday memory with someone else. Ask them to share their birthday memory with you and write down their response.

1. I shared this birthday memory with: _____

2. Their comments about my birthday memory were: _____

   _____

3. The birthday memory that they shared with me was: _____

   _____

Below, draw a picture of your earliest birthday memory. Please label all the people in your drawing.

Assignment

Remember and record your best Easter memory.

Easter arrives every year in the spring. It is the time of year when plants begin to grow, birds lay eggs, and animals give birth to their young. Easter is often celebrated with Easter baskets, egg hunts and an Easter feast at dinnertime. Many of the things associated with Easter are symbols. Many of these symbols, such as eggs, Easter lilies, tulips, and bunnies, represent new life.

Easter is also a religious holiday for many people. Christians celebrate Easter as Christ's resurrection from the dead. That is why crosses are often seen at Easter as well.

Holidays like Easter are celebrated as part of a family tradition. Holidays allow families to have some additional time with each other in order to celebrate. Most adults have a day off of work and children are given time off from school.

As you complete this assignment, think about some of the different ways Easter has been celebrated in your biological home, foster home, and relatives and friend's homes.

My Best Easter Memory

1. My best Easter memory was when I was _____ years old.

2. The following people were present:

   _____

   _____

   _____

3. It was the best because:

   _____

   _____

4. The following items were in my Easter basket:

   _____

   _____

5. The sights, smells, and sounds I remember are:

   _____

   _____

6. When I think about this memory, I feel: _____

   _____

   _____

Directions

Share your best Easter memory with someone else. Ask them to share their best Easter memory with you and write down their response.

1. I shared this Easter memory with: _____

2. Their comments about my Easter memory were: _____

_____

3. The Easter memory that they shared with me was: _____

_____

Below, draw a picture of your Easter memory. Please label all the people in your drawing.

Activity 23   My Best Summer Memory

Assignment

Remember and record your best summer memory.

Even though summer officially begins on June 21 each year, summer vacation really seems to begin the first day school is out. It is anticipated by all, for a lot of different reasons.

Summer often seems carefree. There is no homework to complete (unless, of course, you're in summer school). The weather is warm, fresh fruit is in season, and everyone wants to do outside activities.

Summer is the time for barbeques, vacations, and staying outside until the sun goes down. It's a time when you can spend more time with your friends, attending camp-outs and sleepovers. For these reasons, summer is often a very memorable time of the year.

As you complete this assignment, try to remember the enjoyable times about summer. What are the things that make summer a special time of the year for you? Think about the vivid colors of red watermelon and blue pools. Think about the smell of summer—like hotdogs on the barbeque and the fragrant smell of blooming flowers. Think about the sounds of summer, like the crickets and the ice cream trucks. Think about the taste of summer, like the fresh fruits and the popsicles. Think about the feel of summer, like the cool water and the warm sun beating down on your skin. These thoughts create your summer memory.

Extra-Credit Assignment

Create a list of all of your favorite things about summer and attach it to this page.

My Best Summer Memory

1. My best summer memory was when I was _____ years old.

2. The following people were present:

    _____

    _____

    _____

3. It was the best because:

    _____

    _____

4. The things I did during the summer were:

    _____

    _____

5. The sights, smells, and sounds I remember are:

    _____

    _____

Directions

Share this best summer memory with someone else. Ask them to share their best summer memory with you and write down their response.

1. I shared this best summer memory with: _____

2. Their comments about my best summer memory were: _____

   _____

3. The best summer memory that they shared with me was: _____

   _____

Draw a picture of your best summer memory. Please label all the people in your drawing.

My Best Vacation Memory   Activity 24

Assignment

Remember and record your best vacation memory.

Vacations are a great time to get away. Most vacations are a time of pleasure, rest, and relaxation.

You don't have to travel very far to take a vacation. Sometimes just a change of scenery and a different pace of life is all that is necessary to create a vacation.

Many vacations offer you opportunities that you otherwise would not have. For example, you might try the following activities while on vacation: camping, scuba diving, swimming, amusement park rides, shell hunting on the beach, hiking in the mountains, and horseback riding.

Vacations allow children and adults the opportunity to see new places and experience new things. Vacations help expand your beliefs and knowledge about other places and people. Some vacations take you to a destination where other languages are spoken and the customs are different than what you may be used to.

As you complete this assignment, think about the unique things that you were exposed to that make your vacation memory the best.

Extra-Credit Assignment

Draw a picture of your dream vacation and attach it to this page.

My Best Vacation Memory

1. My best vacation memory was when I was _____ years old.

2. The following people were present:

   _____

   _____

   _____

3. It was the best because:

   _____

   _____

4. The things I did while on vacation were:

   _____

   _____

5. The sights, smells, and sounds I remember are:

   _____

   _____

6. When I think about this memory, I feel: _____

   because: _____

   _____

Directions

Share this best vacation memory with someone else. Ask them to share their best vacation memory with you and write down their response.

1. I shared this best vacation memory with: _____

2. Their comments about my best vacation memory were: _____

   _____

3. The best vacation memory that they shared with me was: _____

   _____

Below, draw a picture of your best vacation memory. Please label all the people in your drawing.

Activity 25   My Best Camping Memory

Assignment

Remember and record your best camping memory.

You don't have to travel very far to go camping. In fact, camping can take place right in your backyard. On hot summer nights, you might not even need a tent. You can just bundle up with a lot of blankets and sleep right underneath the stars.

Maybe your camping memory was a daytime camping trip to the beach, park, or lake. Even though you didn't spend the night, you still had the opportunity to get away, be outdoors, and spend time with friends and family.

Camping usually involves a lot of preparation and packing. Some of the things that are often part of a camping trip include tent, campfire, roasting hotdogs and marshmallows on sticks, ghost stories, star gazing, fishing, and picnics.

In this assignment you will be asked to write down your memories from your best camping trip. What items do you remember packing for your special trip? In which activities did you participate? Did you enjoy the camping experience or do you prefer being indoors, sleeping in your bedroom?

Extra-Credit Assignment

Write a few sentences about "the camping adventure of your dreams." Include where you would go, who would be present, and what you would do on your dream camping adventure. Attach a copy to this page.

My Best Camping Trip

1. My best camping trip was when I was _____years old.

2. The following people were present:

    _____

    _____

    _____

3. It was the best because:

    _____

    _____

4. The things I did while camping were:

    _____

    _____

5. The sights, smells, and sounds I remember are:

    _____

    _____

6. When I think about this memory, I feel: _____

    because: _____

    _____

Directions

Share this best camping memory with someone else. Ask them to share their best camping memory with you and write down their response.

1. I shared this best camping memory with: _____

2. Their comments about my best camping memory were: _____

    _____

3. The best camping memory that they shared with me was: _____

    _____

Below, draw a picture of you best camping-trip memory. Please label all the people in your drawing.

Assignment

Remember and record your best school memory.

On average, you probably spend about nine hundred hours each year in school. That has the potential for a lot of school memories! However, you probably do not remember every moment of the day while you are in school. Rather, you remember the eventful times. These times might be funny, sad, scary, angry, embarrassing, or happy.

In this activity, you will be asked to sort through hundreds of hours of school time in your brain and come up with your best school memory.

Your best school memory could involve good friends, a playground event, a test, a talent show, a report card, a teacher, or something funny that occurred during class. Whatever it is, take time to write it down so that it will not be forgotten.

You might have more than one best school memory. You might even have a best memory from each grade you attended. If so, that's great! Use additional copies of the next two pages and write down your best school memories.

Extra-Credit Assignment

Think of your worst school memory. Write a few sentences about your worst school memory. Include how old you were, what grade you were in, who was present, what happened, and how you felt. Attach a copy of your worst school memory to this page.

My Best School Memory

1. My best school memory was when I was _____ years old.

2. The following people were present:

   _____

   _____

   _____

3. It was the best because:

   _____

   _____

4. The things I did and the friends I had were:

   _____

   _____

5. The sights, smells, and sounds I remember are:

   _____

   _____

6. When I think about this memory, I feel: _____

   because: _____

   _____

My Best School Memory

Directions

Share you best school memory with someone else. Ask them to share their best school memory with you and write down their response.

1. I shared this best school memory with: _____

2. Their comments about my best school memory were: _____

   _____

3. The best school memory that they shared with me was: _____

   _____

Below, draw a picture of your best school memory. Please label all the people in your drawing.

Activity 27

My Best Halloween Memory

Assignment

Remember and record your best Halloween memory.

Halloween is an exciting holiday. It is a time for you to dress up and pretend to be someone else for a few hours. You get to go door to door to collect candy and other treats from friends and neighbors.

The houses in your neighborhood are decorated with scary decorations like cobwebs, ghosts, black cats, skeletons, tombstones, and jack o' lanterns. Some houses are even turned into haunted houses on Halloween night. They might have flickering lights, scary music, and real people jumping out at you while you are trick or treating. Have you ever been scared while trick or treating?

The custom of dressing up in scary costumes on Halloween began hundreds of years ago in Europe. The Celtic people believed that dressing up in scary costumes would scare away evil spirits. They even carved faces into potatoes and turnips and lit them with candles to scare off the spirits. Now we carve pumpkins instead of potatoes and turnips.

Do you believe in ghosts or spirits? Ask an adult what they believe.

Extra-Credit Assignment

Describe or draw your favorite Halloween costume and attach the answers to this page.

My Best Halloween Memory

1. My best Halloween memory was when I was _____ years old.

2. The following people were present:

   _____

   _____

   _____

3. I dressed up as:

   _____

   _____

4. It was the best because:

   _____

   _____

5. The sights, smells, and sounds I remember are:

   _____

   _____

6. When I think about this memory, I feel: _____

   because: _____

   _____

Directions

Share you best Halloween memory with someone else. Ask them to share their best Halloween memory with you and write down their response.

1. I shared this best Halloween memory with: _____

2. Their comments about my best Halloween memory were: _____

    _____

3. The best Halloween memory that they shared with me was: _____

    _____

Below, draw a picture of your best Halloween memory. Please label all the people in your drawing.

My Best Thanksgiving Memory

Assignment

Remember and record your best Thanksgiving memory.

The holiday of Thanksgiving is celebrated each year on the last Thursday in November. It is a national holiday, which means even schools, banks, and government offices close down to celebrate this day of giving thanks.

Thanksgiving is a time to reflect on all of the things for which you are thankful. Unfortunately, many of us take things for granted and don't appreciate the things that we have on a regular basis.

During Thanksgiving, many families get together to give thanks. The focus, of course, is on putting together a great Thanksgiving feast. The feast usually includes traditional foods that date back to the year 1621.

This is the year when the pilgrims celebrated their bountiful harvest with the Iroquois Indians to give thanks for foods and for the Indians who taught them how to raise crops, fish, and hunt.

Many of the same foods we eat today were eaten at the very first Thanksgiving many years ago. These foods include turkey, corn, pumpkins, beans, and cranberry sauce. In this activity, you will have the opportunity to list some of your favorite things about Thanksgiving.

Extra-Credit Assignment

Create a list of at least five things for which you are thankful. Attach a copy of your list to this page.

My Best Thanksgiving Memory

1. My best Thanksgiving memory was when I was _____years old.

2. The following people were present:

   _____

   _____

   _____

3. It was the best because:

   _____

   _____

4. The different kinds of food were:

   _____

   _____

5. The sights, smells, and sounds I remember are:

   _____

   _____

6. When I think about this memory, I feel: _____

   because: _____

   _____

My Best Thanksgiving Memory

Directions

Share your best Thanksgiving memory with someone else. Ask them to share their best Thanksgiving memory with you and write down their response.

1. I shared this best Thanksgiving memory with: _____

2. Their comments about my best Thanksgiving memory were: _____

_____

3. The best Thanksgiving memory that they shared with me was: _____

_____

Below, draw a picture of your best Thanksgiving memory. Please label all the people in your drawing.

Activity 29   My Best Christmas Memory

Assignment

Remember and record your best Christmas memory.

Christmas falls on December 25 each year. Christmas is a religious holiday celebrating the birth of Jesus Christ. Many people celebrate the Christmas spirit, even if they are not religious.

Many children look forward to Christmas because it is a time of festivities and celebration. There are many traditions surrounding Christmas; such as spending time visiting with friends and family; caroling (singing Christmas songs); eating candy canes; hanging mistletoe, stockings and wreaths; gift giving; decorating trees; stringing lights; sending Christmas cards; waiting for Santa; and more.

In this activity, you will have the opportunity to recall the sights, sounds, and smells of the season as you recall your best Christmas memory.

Perhaps your best memory is about a favorite gift you finally received after waiting for it all year long. Or maybe it was how you felt when you watched someone open a gift that you bought for them. After all, Christmas is a season of giving.

Extra-Credit Assignment:

Imagine that you had all the money in the world—but you couldn't spend it on yourself, only on other people. Write down the top five people you would buy things for and what would you buy them. Attach your responses to this page.

My Best Christmas Memory

1. My best Christmas memory was when I was _____ years old.

2. The following people were present:

   _____

   _____

   _____

3. It was the best because:

   _____

   _____

4. The best gift I received was:

   _____

   _____

5. The sights, smells, and sounds I remember are:

   _____

   _____

6. When I think about this memory, I feel: _____

   because: _____

   _____

Directions

Share your best Christmas memory with someone else. Ask them to share their best Christmas memory with you and write down their response.

1. I shared this best Christmas memory with: _____

2. Their comments about my best Christmas memory were: _____

   _____

3. The best Christmas memory that they shared with me was: _____

   _____

Below, draw a picture of your best Christmas memory. Please label all the people in your drawing.

Assignment

Remember and record your best memory from a category of your choosing.

This is your opportunity to complete your best memory from a category that you create.

Perhaps you have a special memory with your mother or father, or a holiday that was not previously mentioned. This category has been created so that you can include any memory that is significant to you in some way. Something very emotional, unusual, or important probably occurred in order for the memory to stand out vividly in your mind.

If you are having a difficult time coming up with a memory that fits this category, consider working backward. Begin by thinking of any memory from your past. Once you begin recalling the events from that memory, try to determine what made it significant or memorable. Once you've determined why it was memorable, complete the title of the assignment.

Other Memory Ideas

My Best New Year Memory, My Best Hanukkah Memory, My Best Passover Memory, My Best Kwanzaa Memory, My Best Valentine's Day Memory, My Best Sports Memory, My Best Pool Memory, My Best Shopping Memory, My Best Recess Memory, My Best "Friends Forever" Memory, My Best Brother/Sister Memory, and so on.

Extra-Credit Assignment

Look up the word "memory" in the dictionary. Write down the definition and attach it to this page.

Directions

Share your best anything memory with someone else. Ask them to share their best anything memory with you and write down their response.

1. I shared this best memory with: _____

2. Their comments about my best memory were: _____

   _____

3. The best memory that they shared with me was: _____

   _____

Below, draw a picture of your best memory. Please label all the people in your drawing.

Assignment

Recognize and record the things that you think about, and identify
which ones cause you to worry.

One of the things that makes us unique as human beings is our ability to think and
feel. We are thinking about things all the time. The things we think about may be
pleasant, unpleasant, or somewhere in between. Each thought can cause us to feel a
certain way. Learning how to "cope" with these thoughts and feelings helps us to be
balanced in life.

Placement in foster care can create a lot of additional things to think about that other
children don't even consider. Some examples include separation from biological family,
attending court dates, learning and following a new set of rules, making new friends,
learning and completing new chores, attending a new school, and making visitation
arrangements with relatives.

In the beginning, it might seem like you are thinking about these things all the time.
But as you learn to adjust to them over time, you will probably find that you think
about them less.

Extra-Credit Assignment

Set the timer for five minutes and write down all the things that you think about
during that time period. Write down whatever pops into your mind. Attach your
thoughts to this page.

Directions

List the top five things that you have been thinking about recently. List your thoughts in the order of the most amount of time to the least amount of time you spend thinking about them. Draw in what you think you look like while you are thinking.

1. _____

2. _____

3. _____

4. _____

5. _____

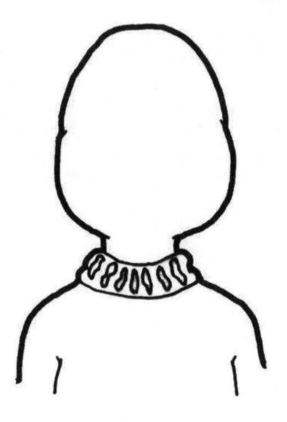

Directions

Answer the questions below.

Do any of the thoughts on the previous page make you worry?

Circle one: YES   NO

If so, which ones? _____

_____

If not, what do you worry about? _____

_____

Talking about your worries with another person can help make those worries feel less upsetting. The other person might offer suggestions for helping you worry less.

Name some people who you could talk to about your worries.

1. _____

2. _____

3. _____

Choose one person from your list and ask them how they handle their worries. Write down what they do to lessen their worries.

1. _____

2. _____

3. _____

Assignment

Identify people who help you and determine the times when you
need the most help.

One of the kindest things that you can do for others is to help them when they need it. Being helpful to others is one way that you can show your appreciation, care, and respect.

In this exercise, the hand symbolizes, or represents, helping others. There are so many positive and encouraging things that you can do to help others using your hands. You can use your hands to hug, touch lovingly, pat someone's back, point someone in the right direction, shake hands, wave hello, and motion for someone to get closer to you.

You also use your hand to indicate when you need help—like when you raise your hand at school. It is important to recognize when you need help and to ask for the help when you need it!

Most adults don't know when you need help. They don't have magical powers that allow them to read your mind when you need help. However, most adults are more than willing to help when help is requested. When you ask for help, you are taking good care of yourself.

Extra-Credit Assignment

List some ways that you could be helpful to others and attach the list to this page.

Directions

List five people who you can count on to give you a "helping hand" when you need it the most.

1. _____

2. _____

3. _____

4. _____

5. _____

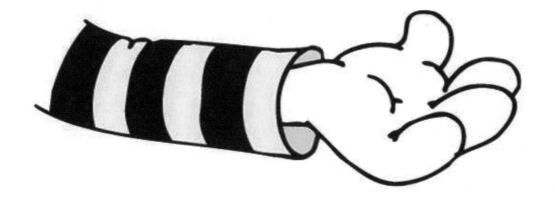

Directions

Answer the questions below.

Do you ask for help when you need it?

Circle one: YES   NO

Why or why not? _____

_____

What is the worst thing that could happen if you asked for help and someone did not want to help you?

_____

_____

On a scale of 1 to 5, how likely is it that the answer you wrote above would happen? Circle the number below:

1	2	3	4	5
very unlikely	unlikely	uncertain	likely	very likely

Asking for help is one way that you can help take care of yourself. Most adults want to help you; they just need to know when and how.

When do you need the most help?

_____

_____

Loving Heart

Assignment

Identify people in your life who love you and who are loving
toward you and others.

"Love" is an abstract word. Abstract means you can't see it or touch it, but you know
it is there. You usually know it is there by a feeling that you have somewhere inside.
People often say that they feel love in their hearts. The symbol of the heart represents
the feeling of love.

During Valentine's Day, the heart is frequently seen as a symbol for love. Most
Valentine's Day cards are decorated with hearts. Many children eat heart-shaped candy
during this time. Some of the candies even have messages of love written on them.

In this assignment, you will have the opportunity to identify people in your life who
you love and who love you back. Try to identify what it is that person says or does that
causes you to love them.

Once you have identified the qualities that contribute toward your feelings of love, you
will need to continue to seek out people with those same qualities throughout your
life.

Extra-Credit Assignment

Design a Valentine-like card for someone you love. Be sure to include the heart symbol
somewhere in the design. Attach your completed card (or a photocopy) to this page.

Directions

List five people in your life whom you love and who love you back.

1. _____

2. _____

3. _____

4. _____

5. _____

Understanding Love

Directions

Answer the questions below.

Is it easy for you to tell someone that you love them?

Circle one: YES   NO

Why or why not? _____

_____

How do other people show that they love you? _____

_____

_____

Love is not only saying the words "I love you." Love is also shown by your behaviors and actions. Your assignment is to show someone else from your list that you love them.

What are you going to do?

_____

_____

Below are some ideas to help you:

give a flower	play a game	make the bed
do an extra chore	carry something	make a small gift
make them a card	put away groceries	write a letter
water plants	sing for them	make a cup of tea

Activity 34　Upset Stomach

Assignment

Identify the things that upset you and learn ways of coping with
those upset feelings.

Have you ever felt like you had "butterflies in your stomach"? Of course you could
never really have butterflies flying around your stomach, but you might feel like it.
Many people experience funny feelings in their stomachs when they are nervous or
worried about something. This is your body's way of telling you to pay attention to the
feelings that are going on inside your body.

Sometimes when children become nervous, anxious, or scared, they might have upset
stomachs. These feelings might be described as a fluttering feeling, a nauseous feeling,
a painful feeling, or a bloated feeling.

Of course, sometimes you are feeling that way because you are really sick with a virus
or you ate something bad. However, other times you might feel sick to your stomach
because something in your life is happening that is upsetting to you.

For example, children might feel upset to their stomachs right before a test, when
adults argue in front of them, when they have to talk in front of the class, and when
they know something bad is about to happen that they have no control over. When do
you feel upset to your stomach?

Extra-Credit Assignment

Draw a picture of the most upsetting thing that has happened in your life and attach it
to this page.

Directions

List the top five things that make you feel nervous, scared, or anxious. Color in the stomach below with a color that shows how you feel.

1. _____

2. _____

3. _____

4. _____

5. _____

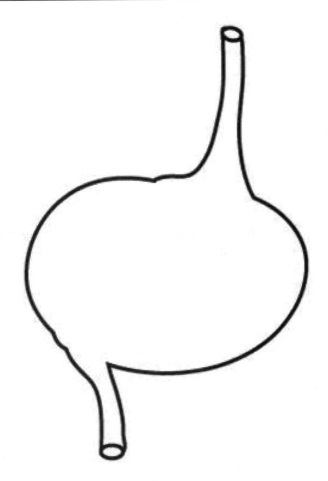

Directions

Answer the questions below.

Do you get nervous, anxious, or scared easily?

Circle one: YES   NO

Why or why not? _____

_____

How do you handle your feelings when you feel:

Nervous _____

_____

Worried _____

_____

Scared _____

_____

Talking about your fears with another person can sometimes make you feel less afraid. The other person might offer suggestions for helping you feel less afraid. Name three people that you could talk to about your fears:

1. _____

2. _____

3. _____

Assignment

Identify the things in your life that you can change, and learn ways of
adjusting to the changes in your life.

Everyone has changes in their lives. That is why learning how to cope with change is
an important skill to learn. Without this skill, life can feel overwhelming, unfair, and,
at times, frightening.

Children in foster care have to deal with this challenge frequently because they
experience so many changes in their lives. Often these changing things in their lives
are decided by others, such as judges, social workers, biological parents, or foster
parents. Most of these are changes they cannot control, like where they live, what
school they attend, or how often they can visit with their family.

Sometimes when children do not cope well with changes, they begin to feel out of
control themselves. Some out-of-control children begin to do things that can affect
their foster care placements, their friendships, their school work, and their overall
feelings of happiness. Have you ever felt out of control?

The key to your success is learning how to adapt to changes and how to control the
things that are within your power.

Extra-Credit Assignment

Describe a time when you felt out of control. Describe what happened, how you
responded, and how it was resolved (or ended). Attach it to this page.

Directions

List five things about yourself or your life that you wish you could change but you can't. These changes could be about your environment, the way you look, or the way you act toward others.

It is okay to feel like you want to stomp around when you feel frustrated. But there are other ways to cope with change.

1. _____

   _____

2. _____

   _____

3. _____

   _____

4. _____

   _____

5. _____

   _____

Directions

Answer the questions below.

Is it easy for you to adjust when things change in your life?

Circle one: YES   NO

Why or why not? _____

_____

What is the biggest change that you have experienced in your life?

_____

_____

Sometimes things change that you have no control over. You have to learn how to deal with the changes. Name some positive things that you could do to help yourself cope with changes:

1. _____

2. _____

3. _____

Below are some ideas to help you:

join a sport	talk about it	write in your journal
listen to music	join a club at school	talk to your counselor
reward yourself	use positive self-talk	make a calendar
	work on a Lifebook assignment	

Activity 36   Clap with Your Hands

Assignment

Recognize five positive things about yourself that make you feel proud.

Each person is unique and has different talents. You probably have many things that you are good at and enjoy doing. One way to ensure happiness in your life is to continue doing the things that you enjoy.

When you accomplish something that you worked very hard at or thought that you would be unable to do, you usually feel proud of yourself. In addition, the people that love and care about you feel proud of you too. This feeling of pride is a good feeling, and it makes you feel like an important and worthwhile person.

Sometimes when you are feeling unhappy, or if many things in life are not happening the way you would like them to, your feeling of pride can lessen. Things that once made you feel good, no longer do.

If this happens, it might be a sign that you are depressed. Depression is a serious problem that can be treated by seeing a doctor or counselor. If you feel unhappy about your life and you no longer feel proud of your accomplishments, please let an adult know so they can help you feel better.

Extra-Credit Assignment

Write about a time that you felt proud of someone else. Who was it? What did they do that made you feel proud? Attach your response to this page.

Directions

List five positive things about yourself that make you feel proud. These things can be about your school accomplishments, talents, or the way you act toward others.

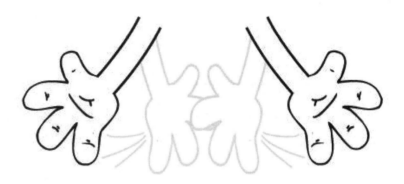

1. _____

2. _____

3. _____

4. _____

5. _____

Directions

Answer the questions below.

Is it easy for you to say positive things about yourself?

Circle one: YES   NO

Why or why not? _____

_____

Choose one positive thing from the previous page and describe how you knew that you felt proud.

_____

_____

Where in your body did you feel proud?

_____

_____

_____

How you feel about yourself is called self-esteem. You can keep good self-esteem by practicing the things that you are good at and enjoy doing. What are some ways that you could practice what you are good at?

1. _____

2. _____

3. _____

Assignment

Select a picture or words from a magazine and write how your feel.

Writing down your feelings is sometimes called *journaling*, and it is a great way to express your beliefs, thoughts, and feelings. Your written thoughts can be kept private or they can be shared with other people.

Journal writing can help you express your feelings, tell your life story, organize your thoughts and ideas, state your dreams and goals, and document the things that take place in your life.

However, journaling doesn't have to be done using written words alone; it can also be done using pictures, drawings, or collages.

In this assignment you will have the opportunity to journal using a picture or words that you've selected from a magazine. This type of journaling is called *Picture Journal*.

When you are looking through the magazines for a picture to write about, try to select one that interests you in some way. You might like the colors or the content of the picture. The picture you select might also stir up different emotions. Just write about what you are feeling. A picture journal entry can be completed as often as you like—even every day if you choose to do so.

Extra-Credit Assignment

Create a folder or binder for your picture journal entries. Keep them in order by date and add new picture journal pages as often as you would like. Make a photocopy of your binder's cover and attach it to this page.

Directions

Cut a picture and/or words from magazines and glue them to this page. On the following page, complete the journal entry.

Directions

Answer the questions below.

The title of my picture is: _____

_____

This picture makes me feel: _____

_____

The most meaningful part of the picture is: _____

_____

because: _____

_____

Other thoughts, feelings, and beliefs about my picture are: _____

_____

_____

_____

_____

Activity 38   Collage Fun

Assignment

Use magazine pictures to identify and explore your current wishes,
thoughts, and feelings.

In this assignment, you will be asked to express your wishes, thoughts, and feelings
through art, specifically, through the use of collage.

A collage is a grouping of photographs, pictures, words, or other objects that are
placed together to create a picture.

Collages allow you to be creative and imaginative in how you express yourself. Your
collage picture can take on a theme such as family time, play time, or school. Your
collage picture can also help you express feelings such as happiness, sadness, or anger.
These feelings can be expressed by the types of pictures you select, the colors you
choose, and the manner in which you glue the pictures onto the page.

Collages can also be used to tell a story about yourself or someone else. You can create
the characters in your story by adding them to the collage picture. What is your collage
going to be about?

Extra-Credit Assignment

Create a three-dimensional collage. This is a collage that include all kinds of objects
such as photographs, fabric, ribbon, stickers, paint, sticks, leaves, flowers (and other
objects from nature), and anything else that you can find to glue.

My Happy Collage

Directions

Cut out pictures from magazines and glue them to this page.

These things make me feel happy!

My Sad Collage

Directions

Cut out pictures from magazines and glue them to this page.

These things make me feel sad!

My Angry Collage

Directions

Cut out pictures from magazines and glue them to this page.

These things make me feel angry!

My Calm Collage

Directions

Cut out pictures from magazines and glue them to this page.

These things make me feel calm!

My Room Collage

Directions

Cut out pictures from magazines and glue them to this page.

These are things I'd like to have in my room!

My Animal Collage

Directions

Cut out pictures from magazines and glue them to this page.

These are animals and pets I'd like to have!

My Fun-Stuff Collage

Directions

Cut out pictures from magazines and glue them to this page.

These are toys and games I'd like to have!

My Yard Collage

Directions

Cut out pictures from magazines and glue them to this page.

**These are plants, toys, and objects
I'd like to have in my yard!**

My Favorite-Things Collage

Directions

Cut out pictures from magazines and glue them to this page.

These are all of my favorite things!

A Collage About Me!

Directions

Cut out words that describe you from magazines and glue them to this page. You can also cut out individual letters to create your own words. Be creative and have fun!

These are words that describe me!

Therese Accinelli, MA, LMFT, holds a master's degree in clinical psychology and is a licensed marriage and family therapist. She has worked with children in foster care for over a decade. Accinelli grew up in Southern California, where she still resides with her husband, daughter, and cat. She is one of twelve children and has an identical twin sister.